Managing Editor
Karen Goldfluss, M.S. Ed.

Editor-in-Chief
Sharon Coan, M.S. Ed.

Illustrator
Renée Christine Yates

Cover Artist
Barb Lorseyedi

Art Manager
Kevin Barnes

Art Director
CJae Froshay

Imaging
Rosa C. See

Product Manager
Phil Garcia

Publisher
Mary D. Smith, M.S. Ed.

Language Literacy Activities

Grades 1-2

Author

Lorin Klistoff, M.A.

Teacher Created Resources, Inc.

6421 Industry Way
Westminster, CA 92683
www.teachercreated.com

ISBN-0-7439-3173-4

©2004 Teacher Created Resources, Inc.
Reprinted, 2004
Made in U.S.A.

Table of Contents

Introduction

Full-Color Language Arts Literacy Activities is a wonderful addition to any first or second grade language arts curriculum. This book was created especially for the busy teachers of young students. The hands-on, developmentally appropriate activities are sure to provide your students with fun-filled learning experiences. The activities are full-color and will add some spice to the regular classroom material. The contents in the book provide a variety of ways to reinforce language arts concepts and skills while maintaining student interest. The activities are easy to implement with little or no preparation at all. The activities are meant to support and be a resource for teachers as they teach these content skills. The activities provide review and practice in the following areas of language arts:

- beginning, middle, or ending sounds in single-syllable words

- short and long vowel words

- rhyming words

- word families

- compound words

- contractions

- synonyms

- antonyms

- parts of speech

- punctuation

- capitalization

- friendly-letter format

- responding to *who*, *what*, *when*, *where*, and *how* questions

- sequencing the events in a story

- sentence and paragraph order

Each activity is set up with an easy-to-follow lesson. First, each lesson states the objective or learning skill and the materials needed. Most of the materials are provided inside this book. Next, the lesson outlines in what kinds of groupings the activity can be implemented. Most of the activities can be adapted in multiple ways and can be "custom tailored." They can be implemented with the whole class, small groups, partners, individuals, or in a science center. The activities can also be adapted for a variety of student levels. Suggestions are listed in the actual directions of the activity or they are suggested in the "Ideas" section. The "Ideas" section contains many helpful hints on such things as storage of materials or ideas to either enhance or extend the activity. Overall, the book is an asset to any first or second grade teacher.

What's the Missing Sound?

 Skill

- Students will identify the beginning, middle, or ending sounds in single-syllable words.

Student Grouping

- large group (Copy appropriate sound cards and or letter tiles for all students.)
- small group
- center
- partners
- independent

 Materials

- chalkboard or whiteboard
- chalk or whiteboard markers
- appropriate set of sound cards (Beginning Sound Cards on pages 5–11, Medial Sound Cards on page 13, Ending Sound Cards on pages 15–19, or Beginning and Final Blend Cards on pages 21 and 23)
- plastic letter tiles or Letter Tiles on page 25

Directions

1. Draw a picture of a dog on the board.

2. Ask students what might be the beginning sound. Write the letter **d** on the board.

3. Ask students for the ending sound of *dog*. Write the letter **g** after the **d**, but leaving a space between the letters.

4. Ask students for the middle sound of *dog*. Write the letter **o** in the space between the letter **d** and **g**.

5. Try a few more examples with other one-syllable words, such as *can* or *cat*.

6. Hand out a sound card to each student. Tell students they will now find the missing letter (or letters) on their card.

7. Have students use the plastic letter tiles or the Letter Tiles on page 25 to place in the missing sound(s). (*Note:* Most of the sound cards have only one answer to the letter box; however, some sound cards may have multiple answers such as those on pages 9 and 11.)

8. Check over each student's work. If correct, give him or her another sound card. If not, ask how he or she arrived at the answer.

 Ideas

- Laminate sound cards and letter tiles, especially if using in a center.
- Use the cards and tiles to aid in assessment.
- Have students create more cards to add to the collection.

Beginning Sound Cards

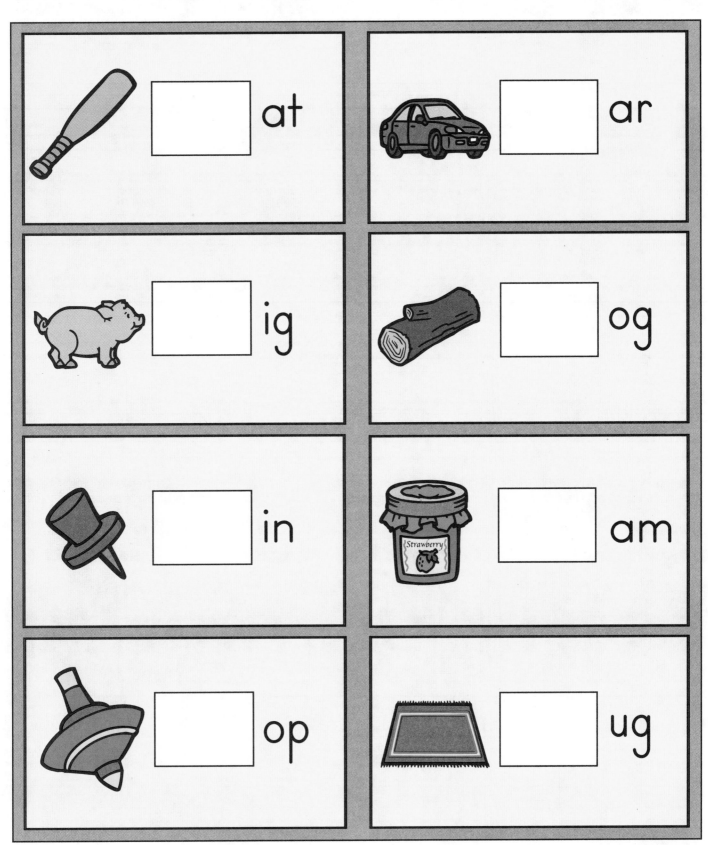

at

ar

ig

og

in

am

op

ug

#3173 Language Arts Literacy Activities

Beginning Sound Cards

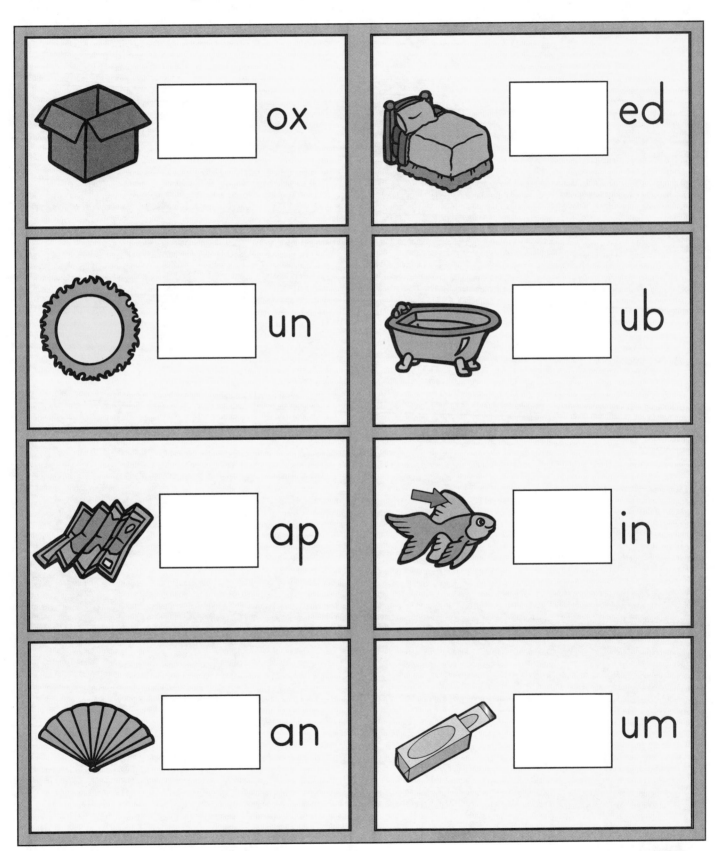

ox

ed

un

ub

ap

in

an

um

Beginning Sound Cards

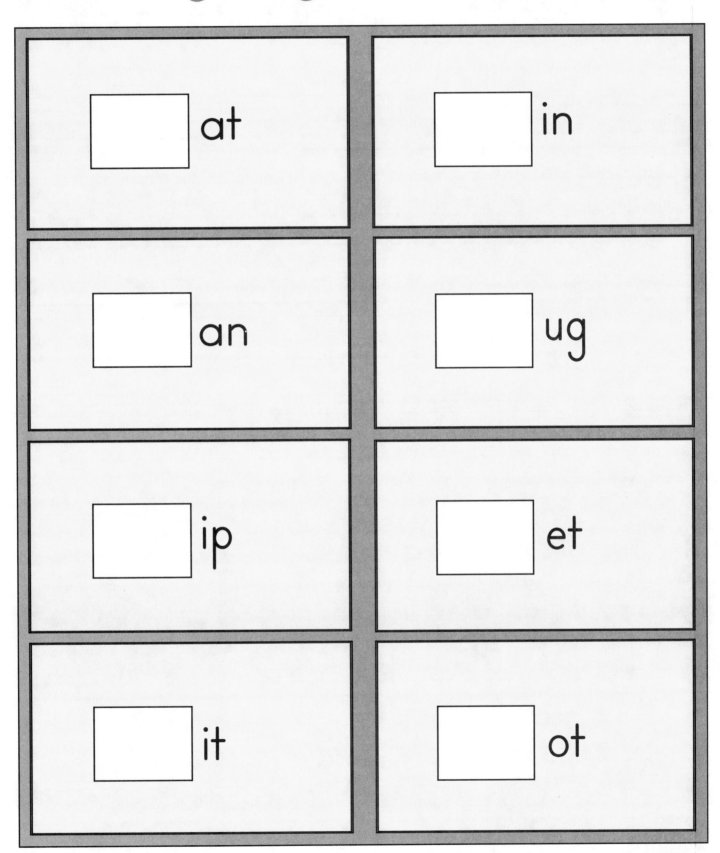

at

in

an

ug

ip

et

it

ot

Beginning Sound Cards

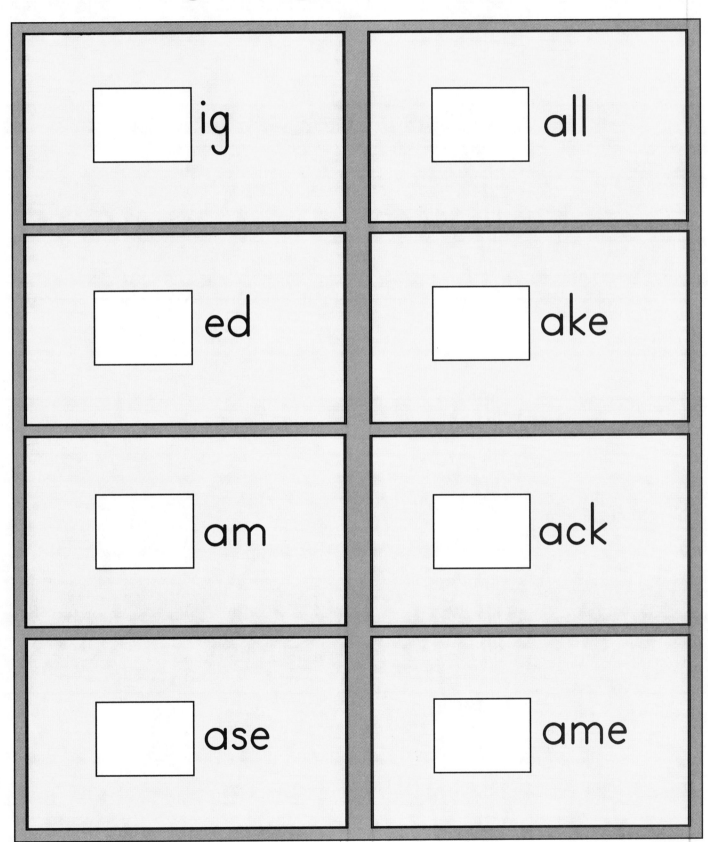

ig

all

ed

ake

am

ack

ase

ame

Medial Sound Cards

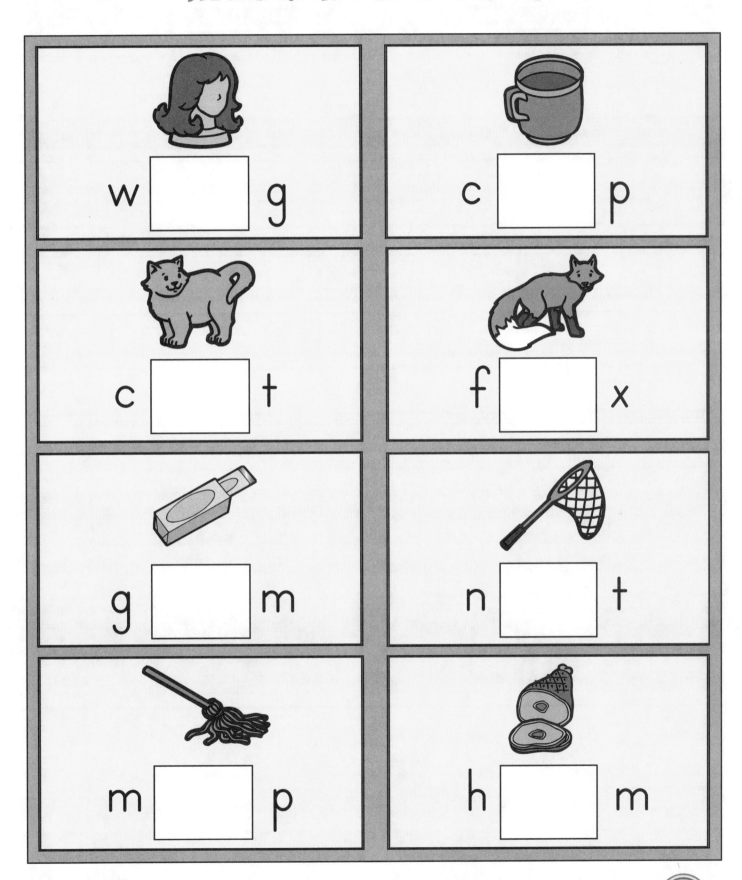

w [ ] g

c [ ] p

c [ ] t

f [ ] x

g [ ] m

n [ ] t

m [ ] p

h [ ] m

Ending Sound Cards

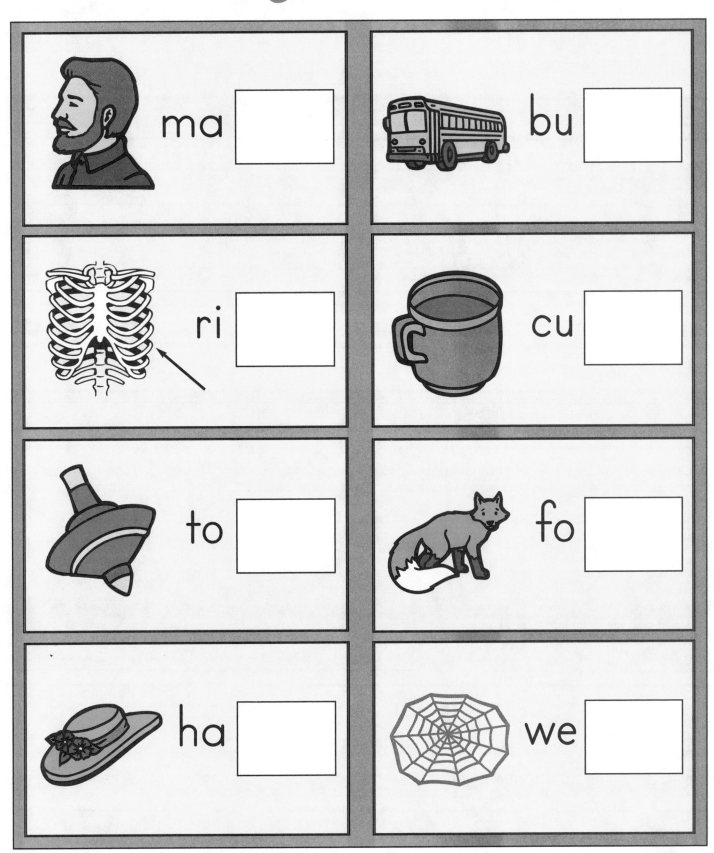

ma ☐

bu ☐

ri ☐

cu ☐

to ☐

fo ☐

ha ☐

we ☐

15

Ending Sound Cards

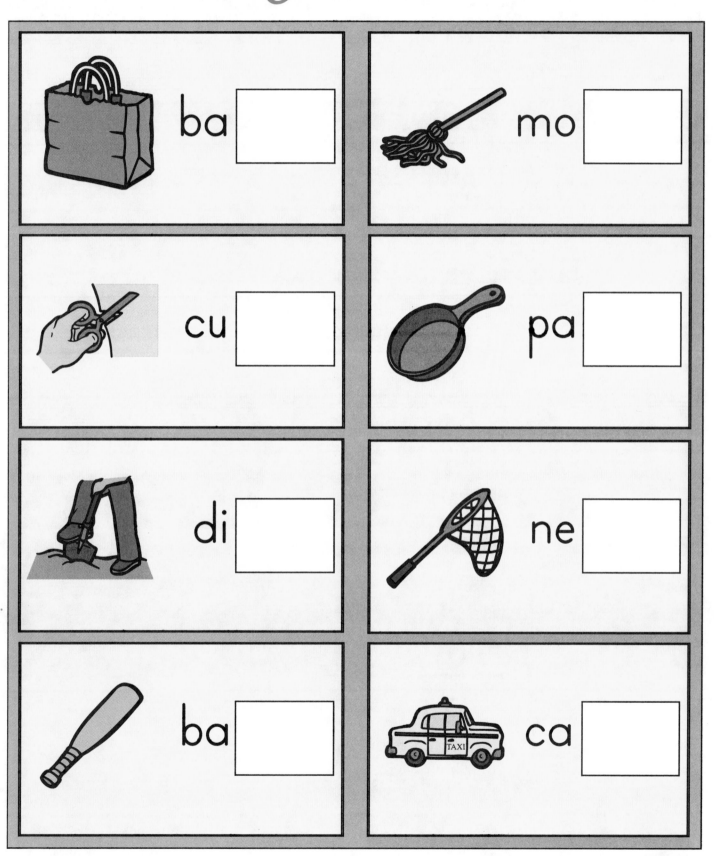

ba ___

mo ___

cu ___

pa ___

di ___

ne ___

ba ___

ca ___

Ending Sound Cards

ba ⬜

mo ⬜

we ⬜

hi ⬜

ca ⬜

ru ⬜

ta ⬜

cu ⬜

Beginning Blend Cards

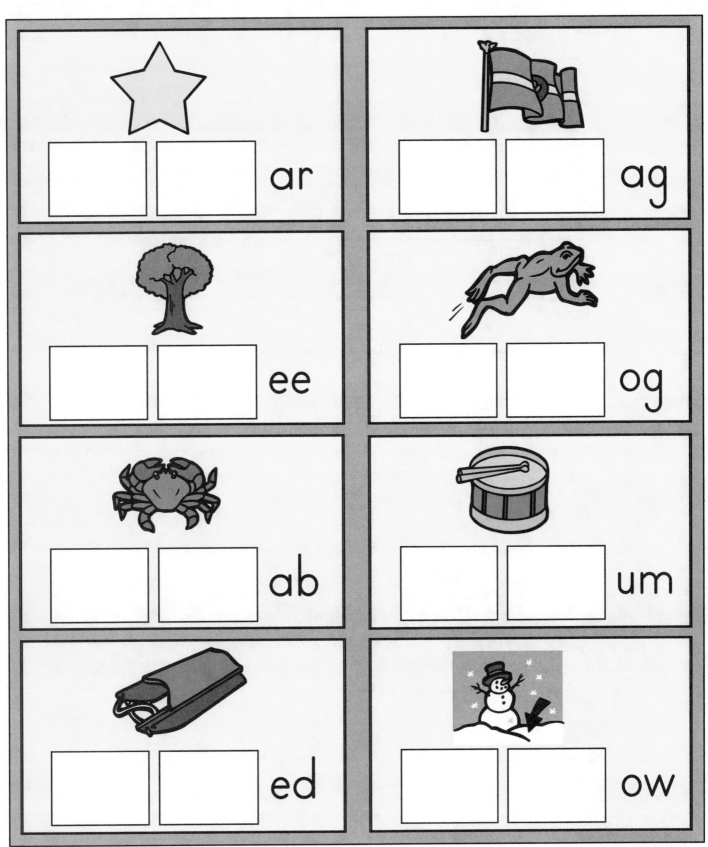

ar

ag

ee

og

ab

um

ed

ow

©Teacher Created Resources, Inc.

#3173 Language Arts Literacy Activities

Final Blend Cards

ne [ ] [ ]

la [ ] [ ]

de [ ] [ ]

fi [ ] [ ]

ba [ ] [ ]

ra [ ] [ ]

mi [ ] [ ]

ha [ ] [ ]

Letter Tiles

a	a	a	b	b	b	c
c	c	d	d	d	e	e
e	f	f	f	g	g	g
h	h	h	i	i	i	j
j	j	k	k	k	l	l
l	m	m	m	n	n	n
o	o	o	p	p	p	q
q	q	r	r	r	s	s
s	t	t	t	u	u	u
v	v	v	w	w	w	x
x	y	y	y	z	z	z

#3173 Language Arts Literacy Activities

Vowel Cookie Sort

 Skill

- Students will identify short and long vowel words.

 Student Grouping

- small group
- center
- partners
- independent

 Materials

- spatula
- one cookie sheet
- appropriate set of cookies (pages 35–53)
- short and long vowel "plates" on pages 31 and 33 (or you may want to label two paper plates "Short Vowels" and "Long Vowels")
- copy of Vowel Recording Sheet (page 28) for each student
- Answer Key on page 29

 Directions

1. Choose from the following sets of cookies: (a) "Short a" Vowel Cookies on page 35 (b) "Short e" Vowel Cookies on page 37 (c) "Short i" Vowel Cookies on page 39 (d) "Short o" Vowel Cookies on page 41 (e) "Short u" Vowel Cookies on page 43 (f) "Long a" Vowel Cookies on page 45 (g) "Long e" Vowel Cookies on page 47 (h) "Long i" Vowel Cookies on page 49 (i) "Long o" Vowel Cookies on page 51 (j) "Long u" Vowel Cookies on page 53.

2. Decide how you want to mix the sets. You may want to have students only sort the "short a" and "long a" vowel cookies. Or you may want students to sort a variety of short and long vowel cookies.

3. Place the appropriate sets of cookies on the cookie sheet.

4. Tell students that they will use the spatula to scoop a cookie off the cookie sheet and place it on the appropriate labeled plate, "Short Vowels" or "Long Vowels."

5. After students are finished placing the cookies on the plates, have them record the words on the recording sheet.

6. The Answer Key is available if you would like students to check their work.

Ideas

- Glue vowel cookies onto thicker paper. Laminate vowel cookies and "plates," especially when using in a center.
- Have students create more vowel cookies to place on the cookie sheet.
- Ask students to write sentences that include words from the vowel cookies.

Vowel Recording Sheet

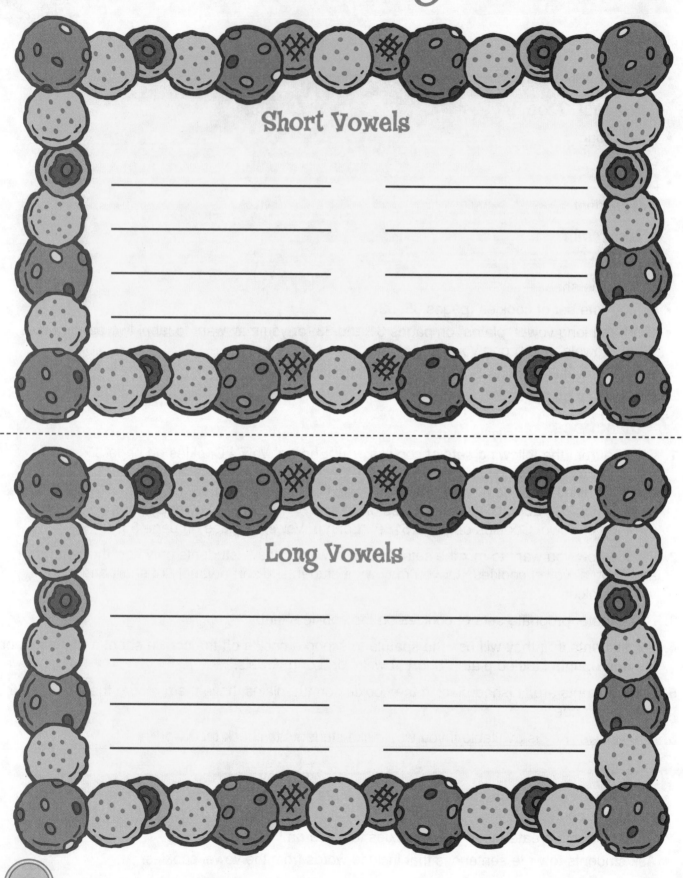

Short Vowels

Long Vowels

#3173 Language Arts Literacy Activities

Answer Key

Short a		Long a		Short e		Long e	
fan	map	make	tape	ten	bed	eat	three
tag	dad	say	date	net	pen	tree	need
ram	cap	race	lake	leg	wet	week	feet
sat	van	cake	ate	wed	desk	sleep	meat

Short i		Long i		Short o		Long o	
big	six	nine	bike	dog	mop	note	old
him	fish	kite	time	pot	fox	road	boat
pin	sit	like	fine	log	hop	bone	nose
wig	hill	five	side	shot	frog	toe	snow

Short u		Long u	
bug	cup	use	glue
gum	rub	June	tube
cut	run	fruit	rule
sun	bus	cube	huge

#3173 Language Arts Literacy Activities

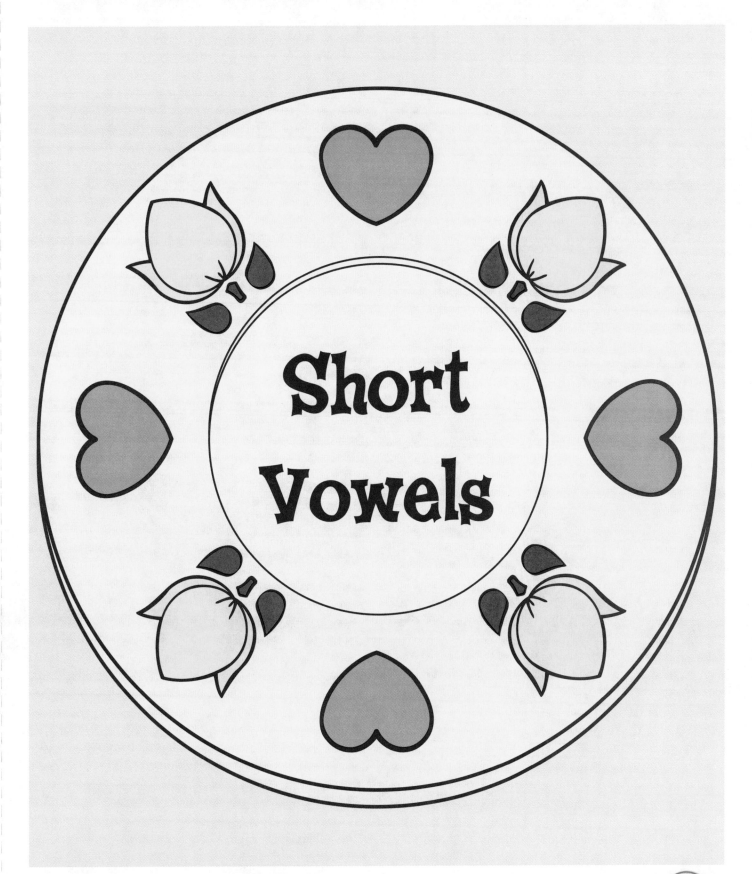

Short Vowels

Long Vowels

"Short a" Vowel Cookies

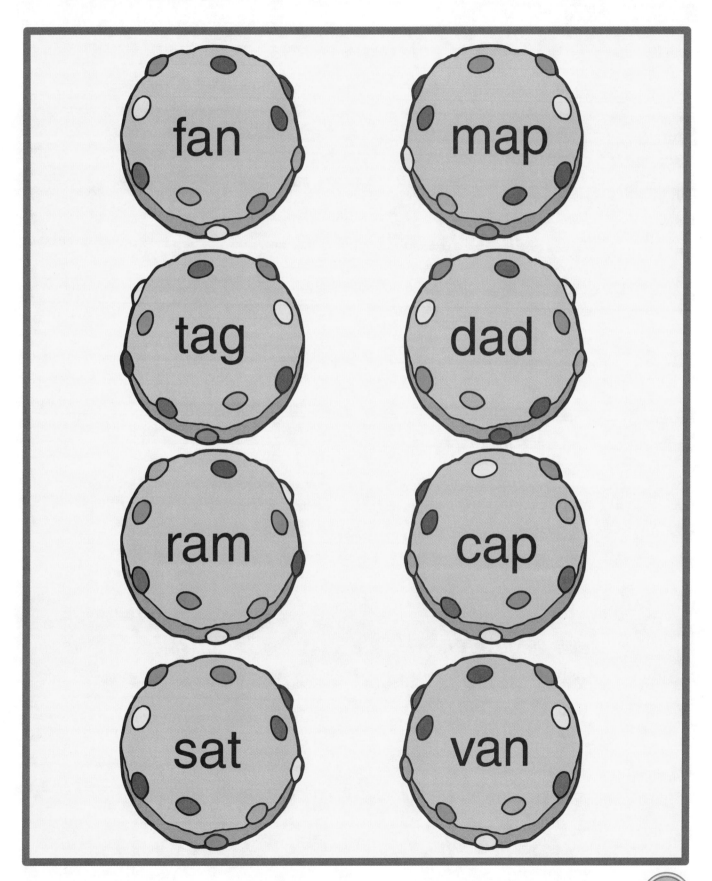

"Short e" Vowel Cookies

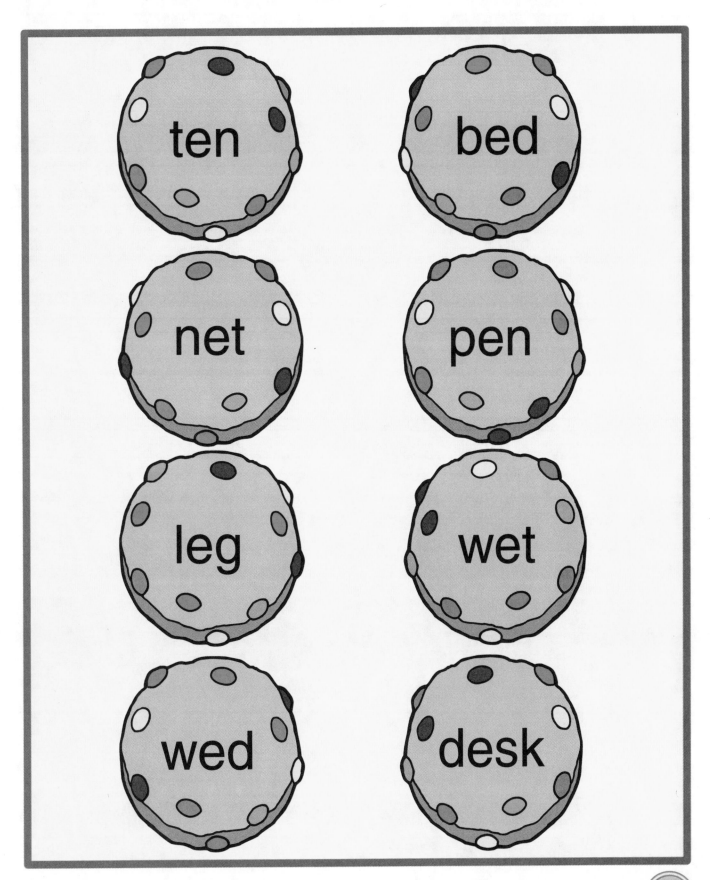

ten

bed

net

pen

leg

wet

wed

desk

#3173 Language Arts Literacy Activities

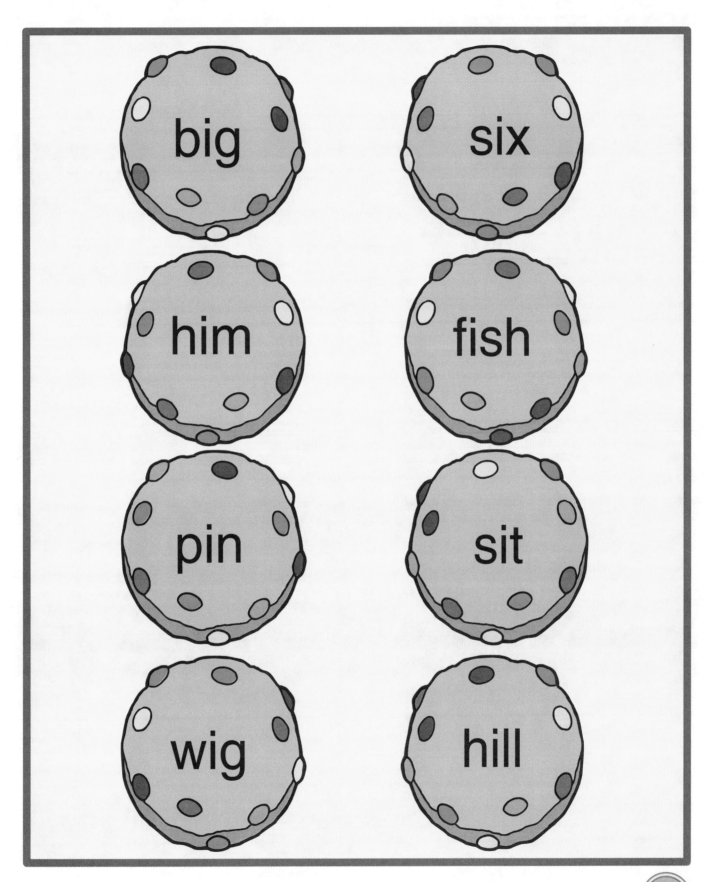

big

six

him

fish

pin

sit

wig

hill

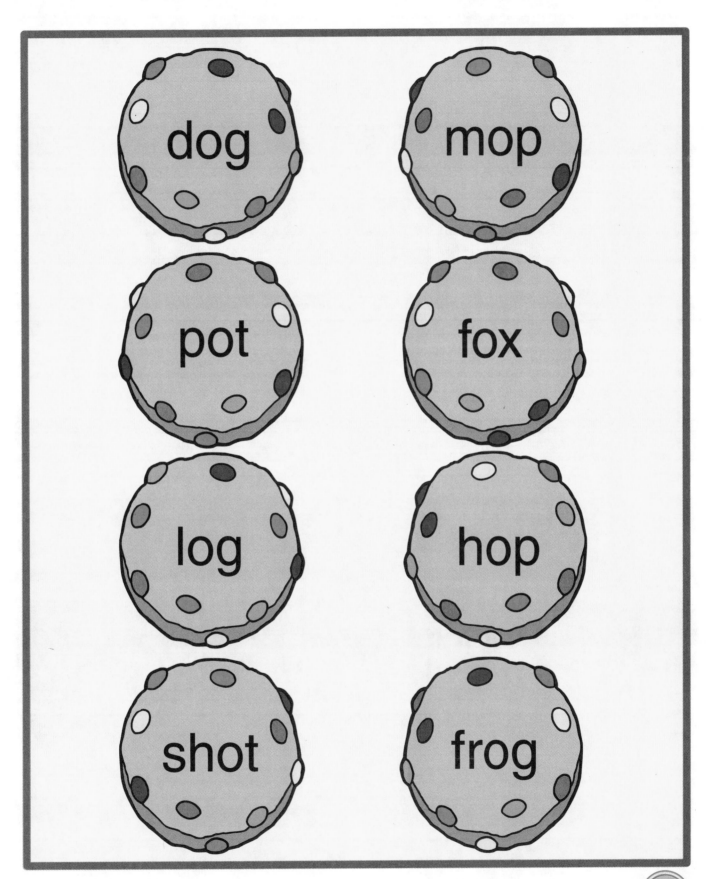

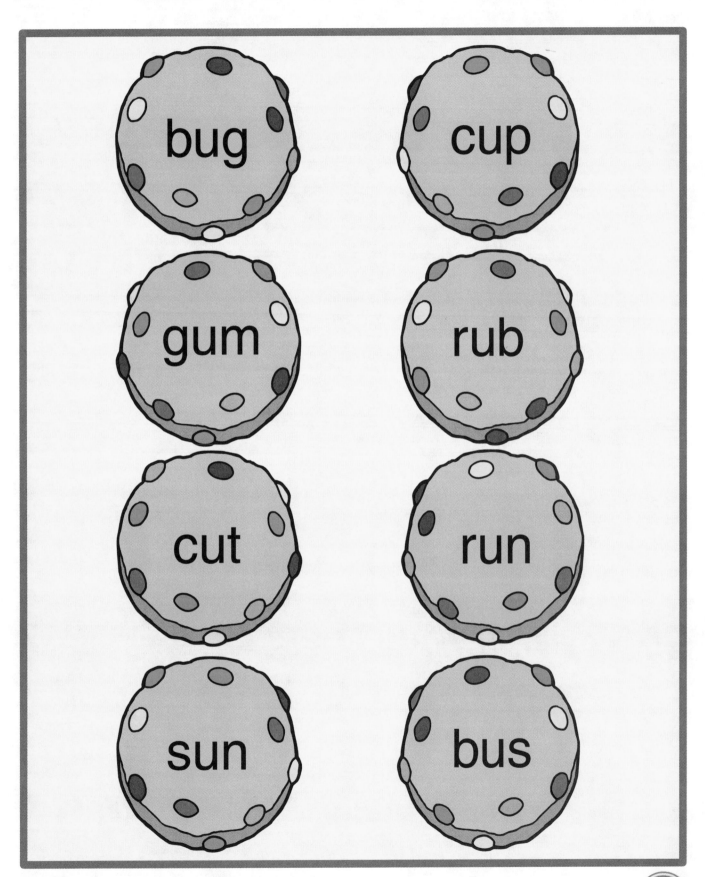

bug

cup

gum

rub

cut

run

sun

bus

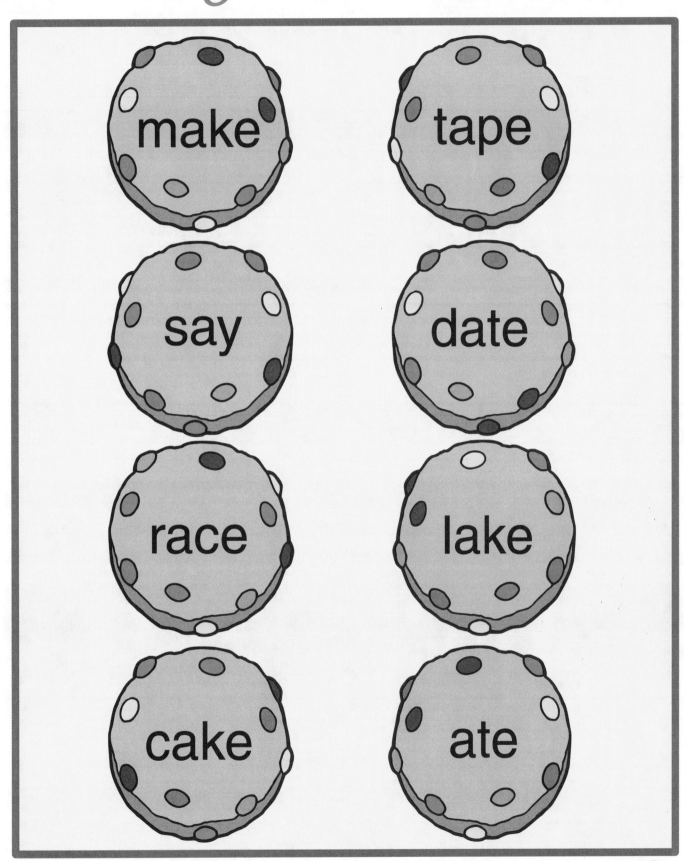

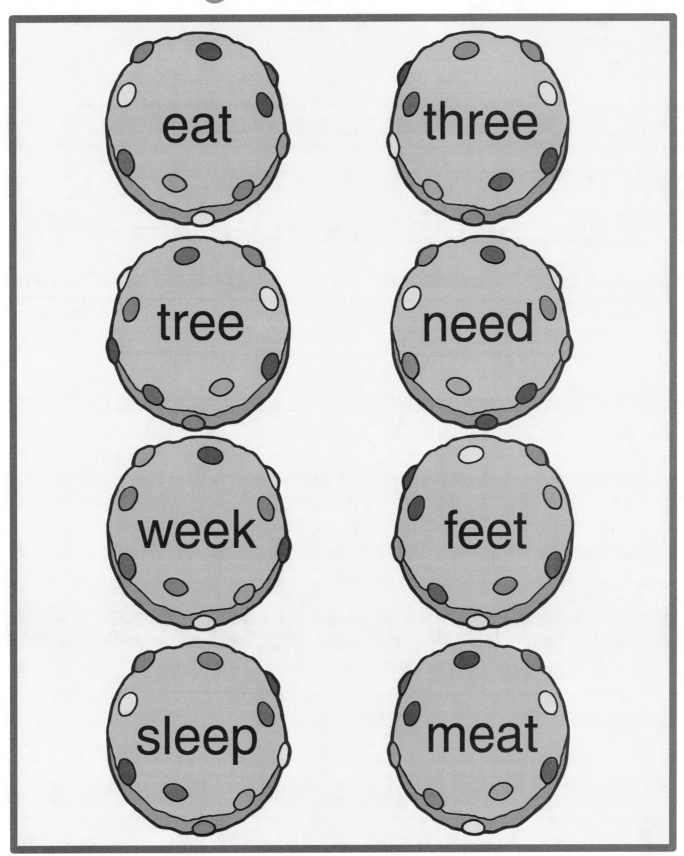

eat

three

tree

need

week

feet

sleep

meat

"Long i" Vowel Cookies

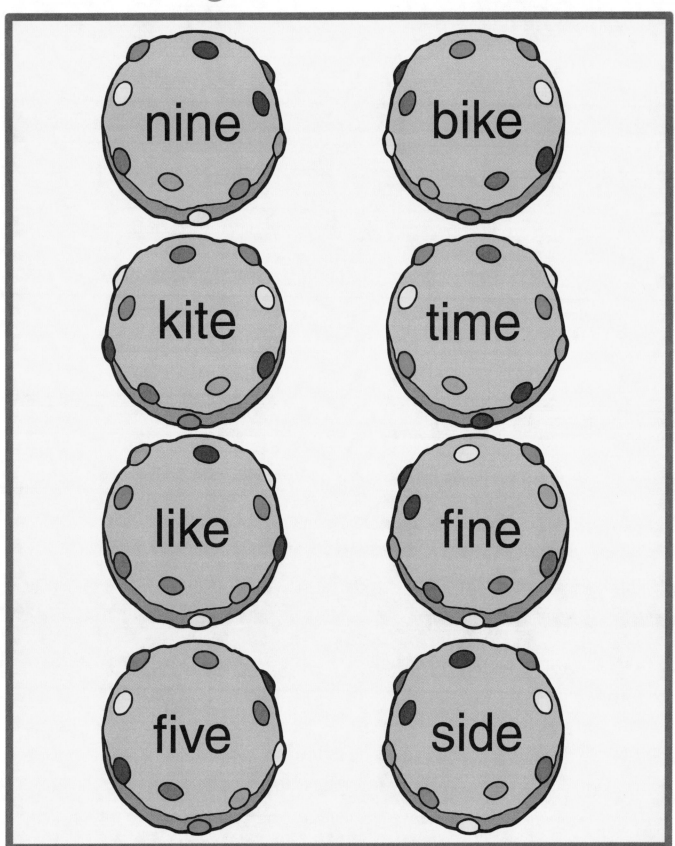

nine

bike

kite

time

like

fine

five

side

"Long o" Vowel Cookies

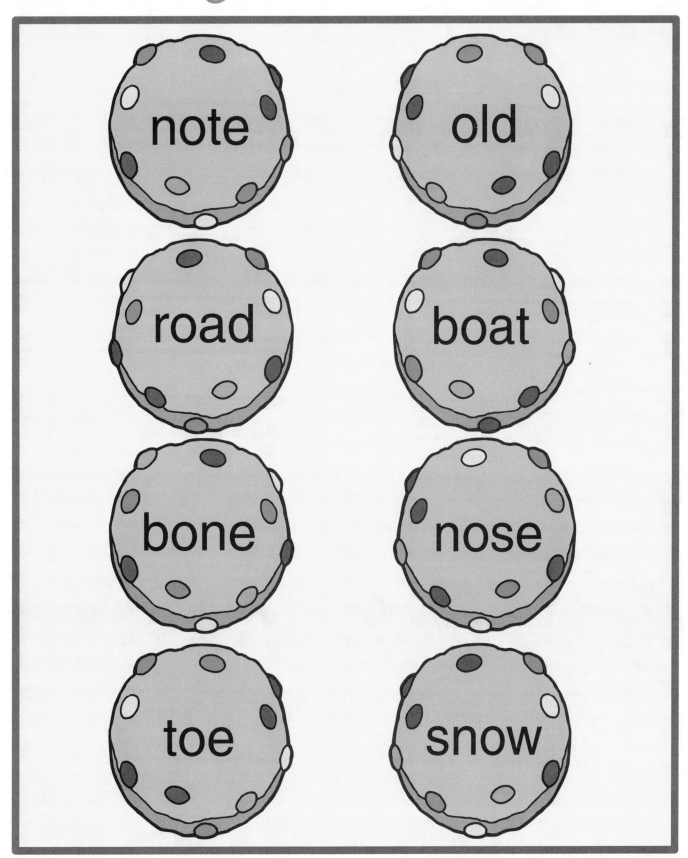

note

old

road

boat

bone

nose

toe

snow

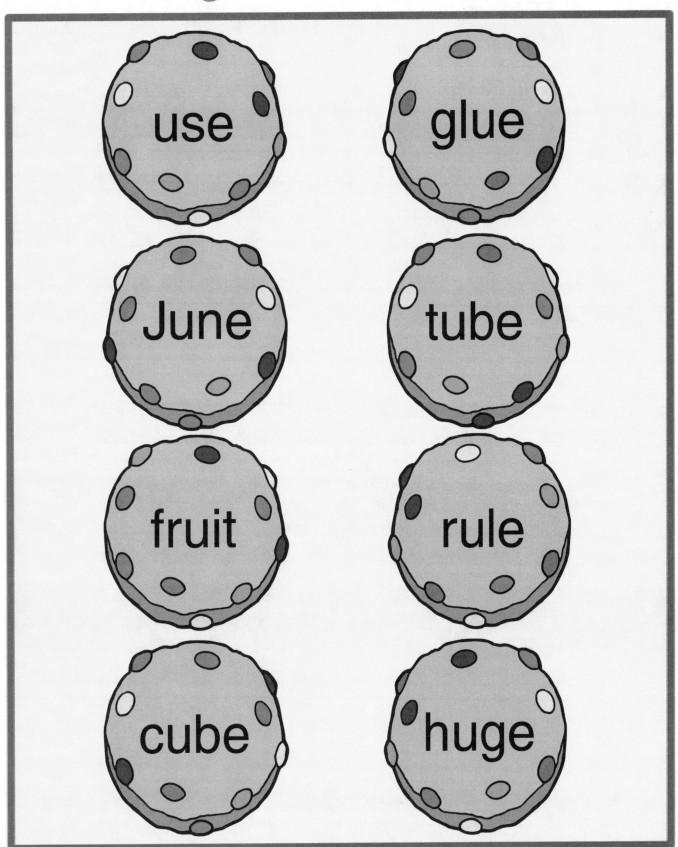

use

glue

June

tube

fruit

rule

cube

huge

Rhyme Time!

 Skill

- Students will identify rhyming words.

 Student Grouping

- small group
- center
- independent
- partners

 Materials

- whiteboard or chalkboard
- whiteboard markers or chalk
- Rhyme Cards (pages 57 and 59)
- Answer Key (page 56)
- paper
- pencils

Directions

1. On the board, brainstorm rhyming words together. For example, write the word *dog* on the board.
2. Ask students what rhymes with *dog—log, fog, hog,* etc.
3. Then draw a picture of man in a van and write the following sentence underneath: The man is in the _____ .
4. Ask students what rhyming word fits in the sentence. *(van)*
5. Place the Rhyming Cards on a tray or in the center of a table.
6. Tell students that they will choose a Rhyme Card.
7. Then have students read the sentence, copy it onto their papers, and then fill in the missing rhyming word.
8. After they have completed all the cards, have students check their answers using the Answer Key.

 Ideas

- Laminate Rhyme Cards for durability, especially when using in a center.
- Have students create more rhyming cards with illustrations.
- Present a rhyming poem each day and ask students to pick out the rhyming words.

Answer Key

 The **pig** has a <u>wig</u>.

 The **boy** plays with a <u>toy</u>.

 The **cat** wears a <u>hat</u>.

 The **fish** is on the <u>dish</u>.

 The **cook** reads a <u>book</u>.

 There is a **star** on the <u>car</u>.

 A **mouse** is in the <u>house</u>.

 A **bee** is in the <u>tree</u>.

 There is a **bug** on the <u>rug</u>.

 There is a **fox** in the <u>box</u>.

 The **king** wears a <u>ring</u>.

 There is a **snake** in the <u>cake</u>.

 The **toad** sits on a <u>road</u>.

 A **cub** is in the <u>tub</u>.

 The **frog** sits on a <u>log</u>.

 The **flag** is in the <u>bag</u>.

#3173 Language Arts Literacy Activities

Rhyme Cards

The **pig** has a _____ .

The **cat** wears a _____ .

The **cook** reads a _____ .

A **mouse** is in the _____ .

There is a **bug** on the _____ .

The **king** wears a _____ .

The **toad** sits on the _____ .

The **frog** sits on a _____ .

#3173 Language Arts Literacy Activities

Rhyme Cards

The **boy** plays with a _____ .

The **fish** is on the _____ .

There is a **star** on the _____ .

A **bee** is in the _____ .

There is a **fox** in the _____ .

There is a **snake** in the _____ .

A **cub** is in the _____ .

The **flag** is in the _____ .

Word Webbing

 Skill

- Students will create words using common word families.

 Student Grouping

- whole group (*Note:* Enlarge Spider Word Web so all students can see.)
- small group
- partners
- center
- independent

 Materials

- Spider Word Web (page 63)
- Word Endings (pages 65–71)

 Directions

1. Make multiple copies of the Spider Word Web for students.
2. Give each student a copy of the Spider Word Web.
3. Place the colored picture of the Spider Word Web in front of students.
4. Choose one of the Word Endings to place in the center of the spider. (*Note:* You may want to use the two-letter word endings on pages 65 and 67 for early readers and the three-letter word endings on pages 69 and 71 for more fluent readers.)
5. Have students write that word ending on their copies (in the center of the spider).
6. Have students brainstorm and write all the possible words which have that particular word ending on the legs of the spider (Example: *–at = cat, fat, bat*, etc.). Encourage students to make real words.
7. When finished, have each student read his or her words to another student.
8. Hand each student another copy of the Spider Word Web and repeat the process with a new word ending.

 Ideas

- Laminate the Spider Word Web and Word Ending cards, especially if using in a center.
- Use the Spider Word Web for other brainstorming activities, such as placing a noun in the center and webbing all the possible adjectives on the spider's legs.
- To extend the activity, have students create sentences using the words on the spider. Tell them to underline the word endings in their sentences.
- Have students make rhyming sentences with their words. For example, "A cat sat on a mat."

Spider Word Web

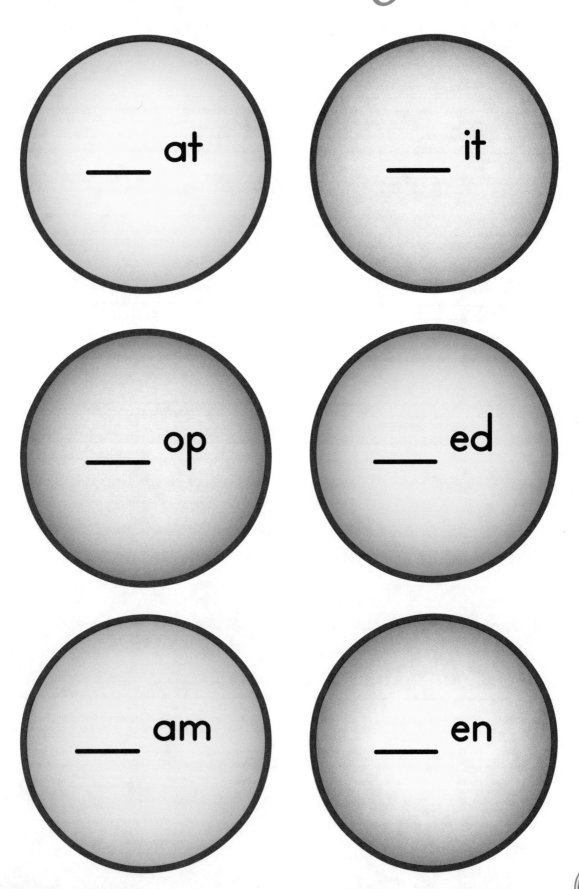

___ at

___ it

___ op

___ ed

___ am

___ en

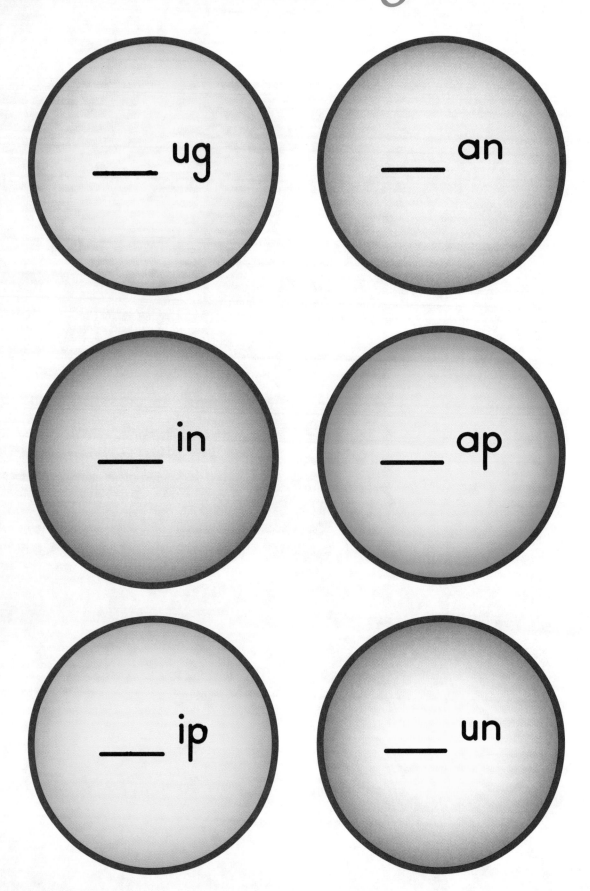

__ ug

__ an

__ in

__ ap

__ ip

__ un

#3173 Language Arts Literacy Activities

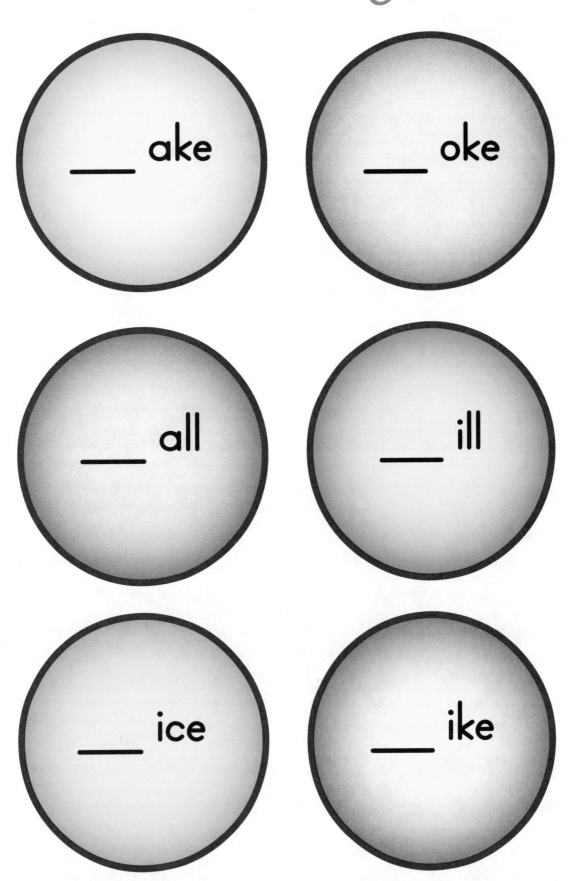

___ ake

___ oke

___ all

___ ill

___ ice

___ ike

©Teacher Created Resources, Inc.

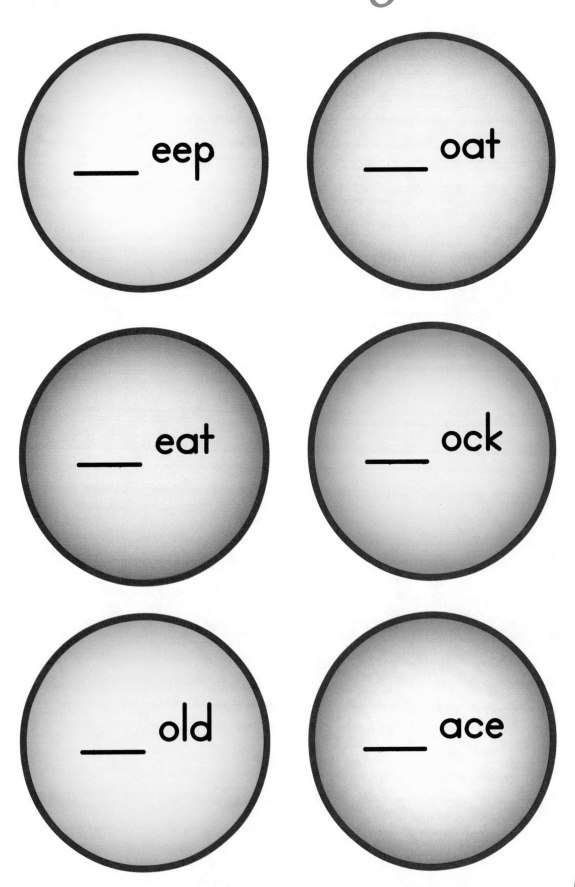

___ eep

___ oat

___ eat

___ ock

___ old

___ ace

Compound Word Equations

 Skill

- Students will identify the parts of a compound word.

 **Student Grouping**

- small group
- center
- partners
- independent

 Materials

- Compound Equations (page 74)
- Equation Board (page 75)
- Compound Word Cards (pages 77–81)

 Directions

1. Copy a Compound Equations Recording Sheet for every student.
2. Give each student a recording sheet.
3. Tell students that a compound word is a word made up of two separate words.
4. Give the students an example. (See example at the top of Compound Equations on page 74.)
5. Brainstorm with students some other possible compound words.
6. Mix up the Compound Word Cards.
7. Tell students that they must find nine compound word equations using the cards.
8. Tell them that they must place the cards on the Equation Board. When they find a complete equation, they must write it on their recording sheets (page 74).
9. Have students compare their equations with other classmates.

 Ideas

- Laminate Equation Board and cards, especially when using in a center.
- Have students create more compound word cards.
- Have students do a search for compound words in reading books, in the classroom, or in a dictionary. Have them use the recording sheet to write their discoveries.

Compound Equations

Example: mail + box = mailbox

1. _____ + _____ = _____

2. _____ + _____ = _____

3. _____ + _____ = _____

4. _____ + _____ = _____

5. _____ + _____ = _____

6. _____ + _____ = _____

7. _____ + _____ = _____

8. _____ + _____ = _____

9. _____ + _____ = _____

#3173 Language Arts Literacy Activities©*Teacher Created Resources, Inc.*

Equation Board

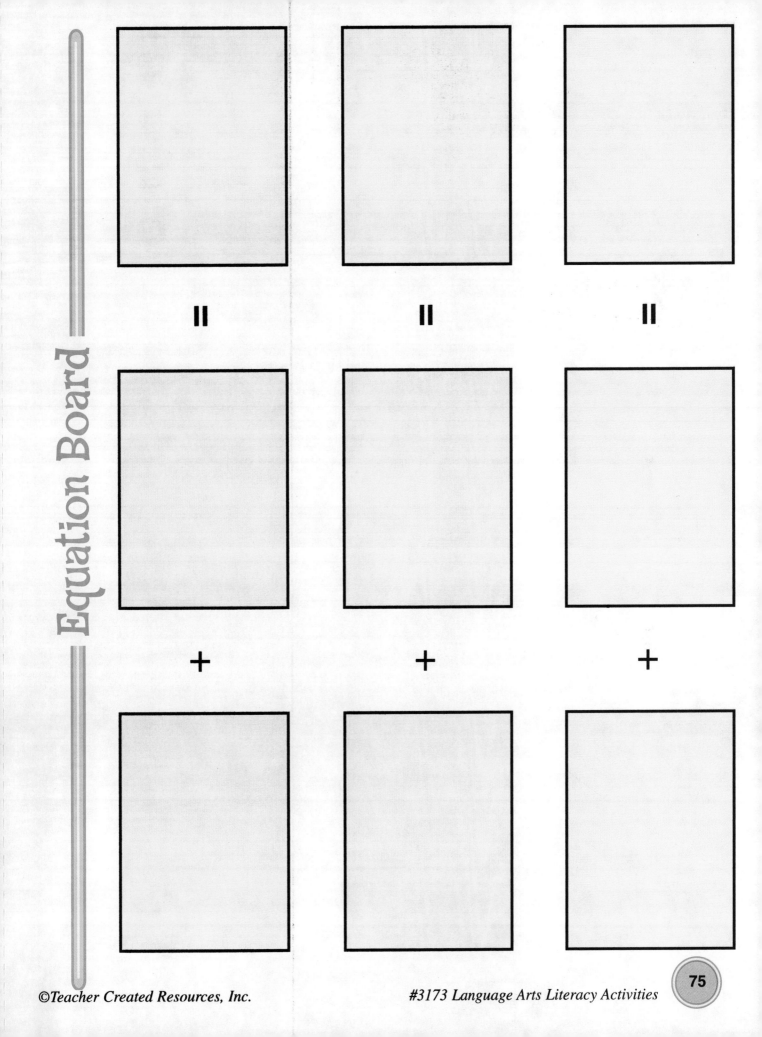

=

=

=

+

+

+

Compound Word Cards

cowboy

classroom

rainbow

boy

room

bow

cow

class

rain

Compound Word Cards

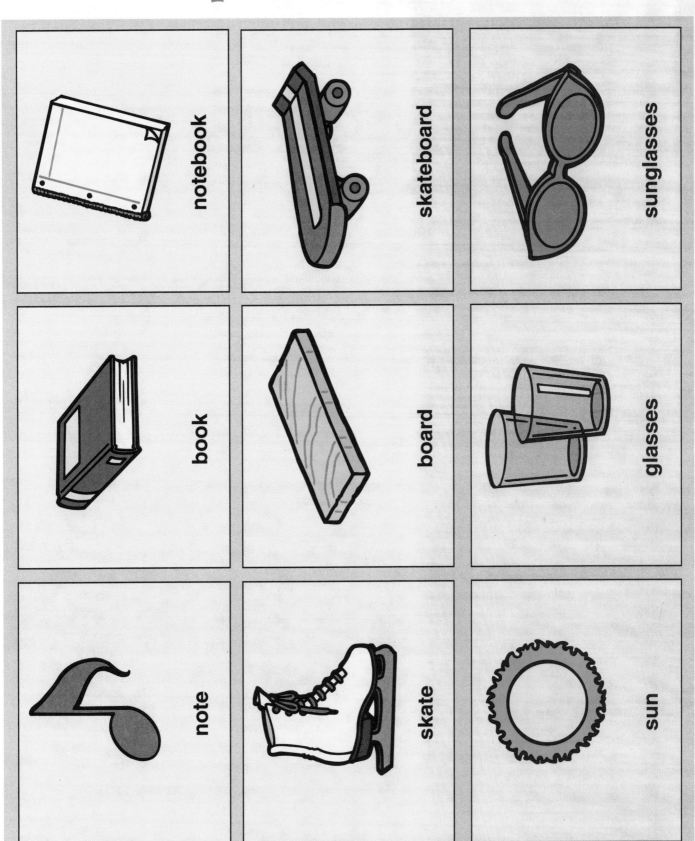

notebook

skateboard

sunglasses

book

board

glasses

note

skate

sun

#3173 Language Arts Literacy Activities

Compound Word Cards

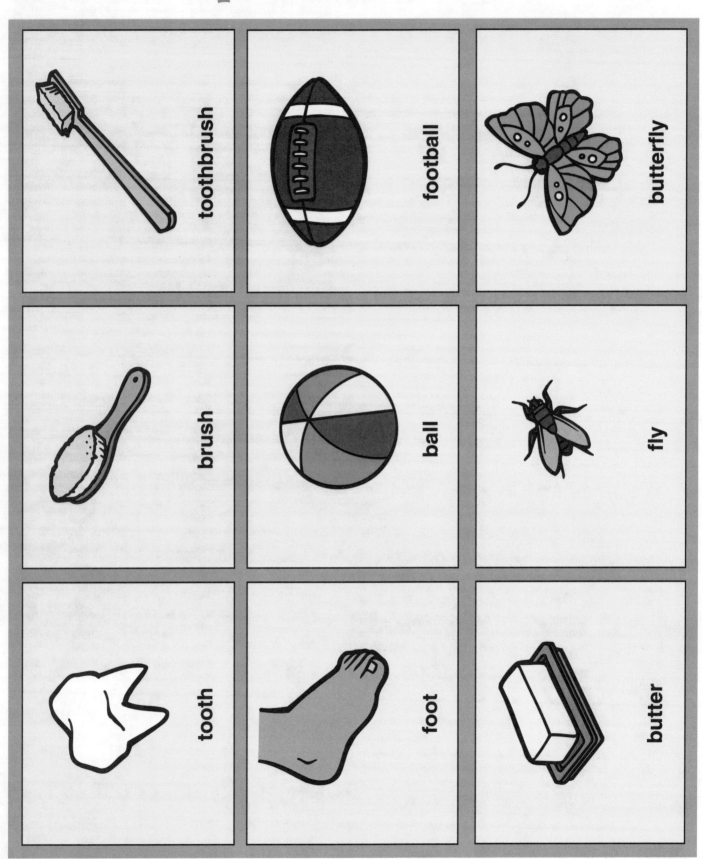

toothbrush

football

butterfly

brush

ball

fly

tooth

foot

butter

Word Detective

 Skill

- Students will identify contractions, antonyms, or synonyms.

 Student Grouping

- large group
- small group
- centers

 Materials

- cards (contractions on pages 87–89, synonyms on pages 91–93, antonyms on pages 95–97)
- copy of Word Detective Recording Sheet (page 84) for each student
- Answer Key (page 85)

 Directions

1. Decide which of the following areas will be the focus: contractions, synonyms, or antonyms.

2. Tell the students on what area you will focus and explain the definition. For example, tell students that they will be learning about antonyms. Tell them that antonyms are words that have opposite meanings.

3. Write an example on the board. For instance, if the focus is antonyms, write the words *hot* and *cold*. Brainstorm with students other examples until you feel they have a good understanding of the area of focus.

4. Tell students that they will become word detectives.

5. Hand each student a recording sheet and a card in the area of focus. Have students write at the top of the recording sheet what they will be searching for (Example: *contractions*).

6. Tell students that they will need to find their match depending on the area of focus. (*Note:* In the case of the contractions, they will need to find two other people who have their match. For instance, if a student gets a card with *let*, he or she will need to find the card with *us*, and the card with *let's*.) When they find their match, they must record it on their recording sheet. For example, *hot/cold*, in the case of antonyms.

7. After recording the match, tell students to mix themselves up. Tell them to switch a card with somebody else. Then have them find their match again and record.

8. Continue until all matches have been found.

 Ideas

- Laminate all cards and answer keys for durability. Store each set of cards with their appropriate answer key in plastic bags.

- Have students do this activity with magnifying glasses so they feel more like detectives.

- Have students create sentences from words on their recording sheet.

- The following is another way to implement this activity: Place one set of cards mixed up on a tray and let students independently find the matches. Have the answer key available for students to check their answers.

- Lay the cards face down on a flat surface and have a matching concentration game.

- Use the contraction cards and the Equation Board on page 75 to create contraction equations. (Example: do + not = don't)

- Have students create more cards for each set.

Word Detective Record Sheet

Searching for:_____

1. _____
2. _____
3. _____
4. _____
5. _____
6. _____
7. _____
8. _____
9. _____
10. _____
11. _____
12. _____
13. _____
14. _____
15. _____
16. _____

#3173 Language Arts Literacy Activities

Answer Key (Contractions)

I + am = I'm

you + are = you're

it + is = it's

he + is = he's

she + is = she's

is + not = isn't

let + us = let's

did + not = didn't

we + will = we'll

could + not = couldn't

will + not = won't

you + will = you'll

Answer Key (Synonyms)

little/small	jump/leap
glad/happy	sick/ill
big/large	keep/save
quick/fast	kind/nice
noisy/loud	mad/angry
same/alike	bucket/pail
quiet/silent	talk/speak
shut/close	start/begin

Answer Key (Antonyms)

begin/end	young/old
start/stop	empty/full
easy/hard	up/down
dry/wet	large/small
hot/cold	kind/mean
close/open	late/early
good/bad	smile/frown
fast/slow	loud/quiet

#3173 Language Arts Literacy Activities

Contractions

I	am	I'm
you	are	you're
it	is	it's
he	is	he's
she	is	she's
is	not	isn't

#3173 Language Arts Literacy Activities

#3173 Language Arts Literacy Activities

Contractions

let

us

let's

did

not

didn't

we

will

we'll

could

not

couldn't

will

not

won't

you

will

you'll

Synonyms

little

small

quiet

glad

happy

silent

big

large

shut

quick

fast

close

noisy

loud

same

alike

#3173 Language Arts Literacy Activities

Synonyms

 jump

 leap

 talk

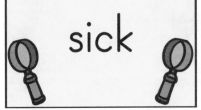 sick

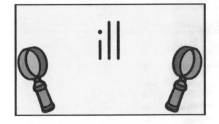 ill

 speak

 keep

 save

 start

 kind

 nice

 begin

 mad

 angry

 bucket

pail

#3173 *Language Arts Literacy Activities*

©*Teacher Created Resources, Inc.*

Antonyms

begin

end

good

start

stop

bad

easy

hard

fast

dry

wet

slow

hot

cold

close

open

#3173 Language Arts Literacy Activities

#3173 Language Arts Literacy Activities

Antonyms

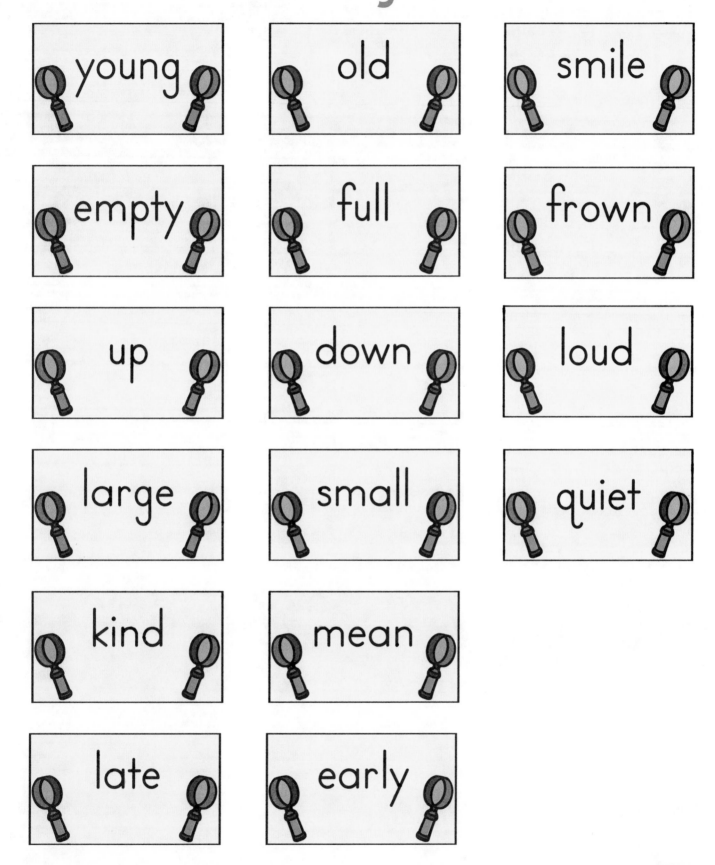

young

old

smile

empty

full

frown

up

down

loud

large

small

quiet

kind

mean

late

early

Parts of Speech Pick

 Skill

- Students will identify parts of speech (nouns, verbs, adjectives, adverbs, pronouns, or prepositions).

 Student Grouping

- large group
- small group
- independent
- center
- partners

 Materials

- appropriate character card (pages 107–117)
- copy of the appropriate recording sheet (pages 101–106) for each student
- appropriate word cards (pages 119–129)
- appropriate Answer Key on page 100 *(optional)*

 Directions

1. Choose the appropriate character card to introduce a part of speech (Nancy Noun on page 107, Annie Adjective on page 109, "Action Verb" Jackson on page 111, Adam Adverb on page 113, Paul Pronoun on page 115, and Penny Preposition on page 117).

2. Post the character card so all students can see it. Read the text on the card.

3. Brainstorm with students other examples of a particular part of speech. For example, if you are working with Nancy Noun, have students brainstorm nouns such as *ball*, *pencil*, *Mrs. Smith*, etc.

4. Hand out the appropriate recording sheet. For example, you would hand out the Noun Recording Sheet if you are working with Nancy Noun.

5. Choose two sets of word cards—the word cards for the part of speech you are covering and word cards for another part of speech. Mix up the cards.

6. Tell the students that they are going to help the character find the words they are looking for. For instance, Nancy Nouns only likes nouns.

7. Read or have a student read a word card. Discuss with the group if it is the part of speech the character is looking for. If it is the correct part of speech, post it under the character card. Have students write it on their recording sheets.

8. Repeat the process until all word cards are used.

 Ideas

- Laminate character and word cards, especially when using in a center.
- Have students write sentences or stories using the words on their recording sheets.
- Have students create more word cards for each of the characters.
- Use the character cards and word cards to display a "Parts of Speech" bulletin board.

Answer Key

Nouns

 dog

 bed

 park

 man

 desk

 book

 girl

 tree

 city

 baby

Adjectives

 round

 tall

 tiny

 sharp

 spiky

 hot

 scary

 deep

 sour

 soft

Action Verbs

 sing

 cry

 read

 skip

 bake

 throw

 eat

 write

 work

 listen

Adverbs

 sweetly

 sadly

 slowly

 quickly

 happily

 loudly

 quietly

 gently

 angrily

 cheerfully

Pronouns

he

we

it

she

I

you

they

him

us

them

Prepositions

 in

 across

 under

 below

 up

 into

 behind

 inside

 down

 over

#3173 Language Arts Literacy Activities

Noun Recording Sheet

Noun: a word that names a person, place, or a thing

NOUN ST.

Nancy Noun

_____

_____

_____

_____

_____

_____

_____

_____

_____

_____

Adjective Recording Sheet

Adjective: a word that describes a noun or pronoun

Annie Adjective

_____

_____

_____

_____

_____

_____

_____

_____

_____

_____

#3173 Language Arts Literacy Activities

Action Verb Recording Sheet

Action Verb: a word that shows action or tells what something is doing

"Action Verb"
Jackson

_____

_____

_____

_____

_____

_____

_____

_____

_____

Adverb Recording Sheet

Adverb: a word that describes a verb, an adjective, or another adverb

Adam Adverb

Pronoun Recording Sheet

Pronoun: a word that takes the place of a noun

Paul Pronoun

_____

_____

_____

_____

_____

_____

_____

_____

_____

_____

_____

Preposition Recording Sheet

Preposition: a word that shows a position or direction

Penny Preposition

_____

_____

_____

_____

_____

_____

_____

_____

_____

#3173 Language Arts Literacy Activities

I like words that are nouns.

A noun is a word that names

a person, a place, or a thing.

#3173 Language Arts Literacy Activities

I only like words that are adjectives. An adjective is a word that describes a noun or pronoun.

#3173 Language Arts Literacy Activities

"Action Verb" Jackson

I only like words that are action verbs. An action verb is a word that shows action or tells what something is doing.

I only like words that are adverbs. An adverb is a word that describes a verb, an adjective, or another adverb.

I only like words that are pronouns. A pronoun is a word that takes the place of a noun.

I only like words that are prepositions. A preposition is a word that shows a position or direction.

118

Nouns

dog

bed

park

man

desk

book

girl

tree

city

baby

Adjectives

round

tall

tiny

sharp

spiky

hot

scary

deep

sour

soft

#3173 Language Arts Literacy Activities

Action Verbs

sing

cry

read

skip

bake

throw

eat

write

work

listen

#3173 Language Arts Literacy Activities

Adverbs

 sweetly

 sadly

 slowly

 quickly

 happily

 loudly

 quietly

 gently

 angrily

 cheerfully

#3173 Language Arts Literacy Activities

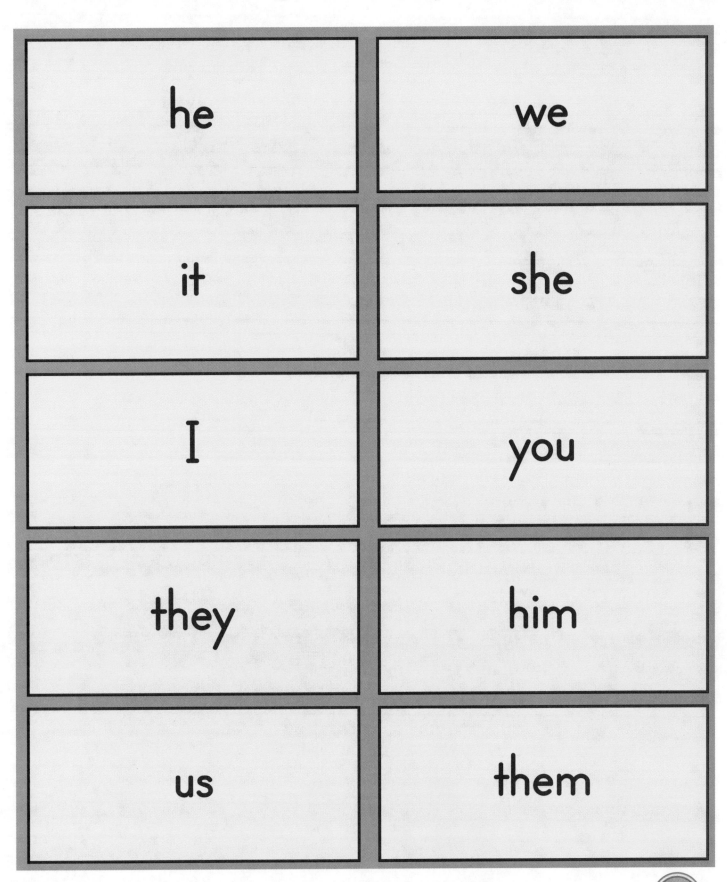

he	we
it	she
I	you
they	him
us	them

Prepositions

in

across

under

below

up

into

behind

inside

down

over

#3173 Language Arts Literacy Activities

Put on the Teacher's Hat

Skill

- Students will use basic knowledge of punctuation and capitalization rules.

Student Grouping

- large group (*Note:* Make multiple copies of Correction Cards.)
- small group
- center
- partners
- independent

Materials

- chalkboard or whiteboard
- chalk or whiteboard markers
- appropriate set of Correction Cards (pages 133–141)
- paper and pencils
- appropriate Answer Key (page 132)

Directions

1. Write a sentence incorrectly on the board. (Example: i went to the store)

2. Ask the students what is wrong in the sentence. (The letter *i* should be capitalized and there should be a period at the end of the sentence.)

3. Brainstorm with students things that they need to remember when writing sentences. (Examples: capitalize first word in a sentence, capitalize names of people and places, place the correction punctuation mark at the end of the sentence, etc.)

4. Tell them that today they will become teachers and will help some students with their sentences (or paragraphs).

5. Pick the appropriate set of cards: Correction Cards 1 (basic capitalization and end marks in a sentence), Correction Cards 2 (basic capitalization and punctuation, including commas and quotation marks, in a sentence), Correction Cards 3 (basic capitalization and punctuation, including commas/apostrophes/quotation marks, in a paragraph). Give each student one Correction Card (or copy whole page). (*Note:* You can also post them in a center or cut them up and place on a tray for students to pick.)

6. Then have them study that student's sentence (or paragraph). Tell them that there are mistakes in the sentence that the student wrote. The number of mistakes is located on the tip of the pencil.

7. Tell students to write the name of the student on their papers (located to the left of each pencil) and then rewrite the sentence (or paragraph) correctly next to the name of the student. (*Optional:* Have students use the Answer Key to check their sentences.)

Ideas

- Laminate Correction Cards for durability.
- Add more Correction Cards by taking sample sentences with errors from students' work.
- Make it a habit to have students "play teacher" when they read each other's work or journal.

Answer Key (Set 1)

 Sue — I like to eat pizza.

 Dave — Do you want to play?

 Ron — My name is Ron.

 Mark — Today is Saturday.

 Kate — How old are you?

 Bob — Look out for the tree!

 Jake — Sparky is my dog.

 Mike — When is the game?

 Lisa — Give me the ball.

 Sara — It is hot in July.

 Tim — I like Ben.

 Rose — That was hot!

Answer Key (Set 2)

 Marcie — I ate peas, chips, and bread.

 Judy — Do you think John is coming?

 Sally — Sam asked, "Where is Tom?"

 Peter — I play soccer, tennis, and football.

 James — I saw Joe on Wattle Street.

 Tony — We are leaving next Monday.

 Denise — Do you live in Chicago?

 Rich — The teacher said, "I will help you."

 Jose — All trees have leaves, bark, and roots.

 Jenny — My mom asked, "Who is your friend?"

 Frank — My friends are Jake, John, and Sue.

 Wendi — Sue yelled, "Stop it!"

Answer Key (Set 3)

 Thomas

I love a big, fat chair! I can curl up in a big, fat chair and read a book. I can take a nap in a big, fat chair. I can't think of a better place to be than in a big, fat chair!

 Alicia

I crushed a car! I didn't mean to. I was running into the house and my little brother's tiny plastic car was in the way. I stepped on it and crushed it. He cried, "You are mean!" I have to buy him a new car.

 Pat

I love dessert! There are so many choices. There are cookies, cake, pie, and ice cream. I think brownies are my favorite. I wish I could just eat desserts and never spinach!

Jason

I don't like sodas. When I finish drinking one of them, I burp. People would say, "That is rude." Sometimes when I open one, it sprays all over the place. I think I'll just drink water.

Correction Cards (Set 1)

 Sue: i like to eat pizza 2

 Dave: do you want to play 2

 Ron: my name is ron. 2

 Mark: Today is saturday 2

 Kate: how old are you 2

 Bob: look out for the tree 2

#3173 Language Arts Literacy Activities

©*Teacher Created Resources, Inc.*

Correction Cards (Set 1)

 Jake — sparky is my dog 2

 Mike — when is the game 2

 Lisa — give me the ball 2

 Sara — it is hot in July 2

 Tim — i like ben. 2

 Rose — that was hot 2

#3173 Language Arts Literacy Activities

Correction Cards (Set 2)

 Marcie

i ate peas chips, and bread. **2**

 Judy

do you think john is coming **3**

 Sally

Sam asked, "Where is tom **3**

 Peter

I play soccer tennis, and football **2**

 James

I saw joe on wattle street. **3**

 Tony

we are leaving next monday **3**

#3173 Language Arts Literacy Activities

Correction Cards (Set 2)

 Denise | do you live in chicago 3

 Rich | The teacher said, i will help you 4

 Jose | All trees have leaves bark, and roots 2

 Jenny | My mom asked, who is your friend 4

 Frank | My friends are jake john, and sue 5

 Wendi | Sue yelled, Stop it 3

#3173 Language Arts Literacy Activities

Correction Cards (Set 3)

Thomas

I love a big, fat chair! i can curl up in a big, fat chair and read a book   I can take a nap in a big fat chair. I can t think of a better place to be than in a big, fat chair!

4

Alicia

I crushed a car! i didn t mean to. I was running into the house and my little brother's tiny plastic car was in the way   I stepped on it and crushed it. He cried, You are mean! I have to buy him a new car.

5

Pat

I love dessert! there are so many choices. There are cookies cake pie, and ice cream. I think brownies are my favorite   I wish I could just eat desserts and never spinach!

4

Jason

I don't like sodas. When I finish drinking one of them, I burp People would say,   That is rude." Sometimes when I open one, it sprays all over the place. I think I ll just drink water

4

A Letter to a Friendly Monster

Skill

- Students will write a friendly letter with the date, salutation, body, closing, and signature.

Student Grouping

- large group
- small group
- center
- independent

Materials

- a copy of a blank letter form for each student (page 144)
- Friendly Letter (page 145) posted where students can see or make a copy for each student
- Friendly Monsters (page 147)

Directions

1. Ask students if any of them has received a letter. Ask them the following questions: What was on the letter? Who was it from? How did you know? How was it written? What did it say?

2. Show students Friendly Letter. Tell them that this is way to write a friendly letter. Review the parts of the letter with students. Write on the board examples of greetings and closings.

3. Give each student a blank letter form.

4. Tell students that they are going to write a letter to a friendly monster.

5. Show students the page with the different friendly monsters. Go over each one.

6. Have students choose one monster and write a letter to it. Have them write about a specific topic (describing their day at school, their family, a trip they took, etc.). Encourage students to brainstorm ideas before writing their letters.

7. Have students each write a letter and then show it to a friend for proofing.

8. Collect letters for review.

Ideas

- Laminate Friendly Letter and the pictures of the friendly monsters for durability.
- Create addresses for each of the monsters, and have students address envelopes to the monsters.
- If there is time, answer the letters from the students as if you were the friendly monster or have an older class do it.
- Place the blank letter form in a writing center so students can write letters to their friends or other people.

_____

_____,

_____

_____

_____

_____

_____

_____

_____

_____

_____

_____,

_____

Friendly Letter

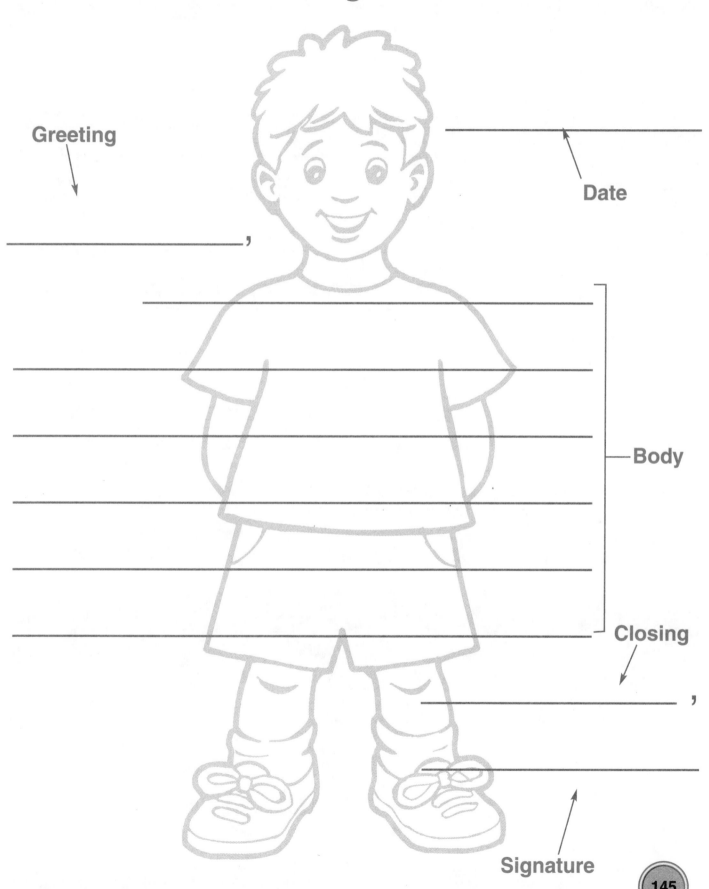

Greeting

_____ ,

Date

Body

Closing

_____ ,

_____

Signature

Friendly Monsters

Boomer

Freesha

Juju

Himie

Winky

Garf

#3173 Language Arts Literacy Activities

Read, Respond, and Sequence!

Skills

- Students will respond to *who, what, when, where,* and *how* questions.
- Students will sequence the events in a story.

Student Grouping

- large group
- small group
- center
- independent

Materials

- Comprehension Card (page 151, page 155, or page 159)
- matching Sequence Cards (page 153, page 157, or page 161)
- pencil and paper

Directions

1. Pick the Comprehension Card and Sequence Cards that match your students' reading levels. (*Note:* Fonts vary according to reading levels.)
2. Make a copy of the Comprehension Card and Sequence Cards for each student.
3. Have students look at the title and picture on the Comprehension Card.
4. Ask students what they think the story will be about.
5. Read the story together or have students read the story independently or in partners.
6. Have students read the questions below the story. (*Note:* For early readers, read the questions together.)
7. Have them record their answers on a piece of paper and discuss them. (*Note:* Answers are located on the back of the card.)
8. Put the Comprehension Cards away.
9. Cut out the Sequence Cards and mix them up.
10. Have students read the text on each Sequence Card.
11. Have students put the Sequence Cards in order of the story.
12. Check the order in which each student placed the cards.

Ideas

- Laminate the Comprehension Cards and Sequence Cards for durability.
- Store each Comprehension Card and its matching Sequence Cards in a large, plastic bag.
- To practice using a Table of Contents, an extra Comprehension Card on page 163 is included.

Comprehension Card

Directions: Read the story and answer the questions.

A Bath

I scrub myself in the tub. A bug looks at me.
I splash on the rug. The bug jumps in the tub.

1. Where is the person?

2. What looks at him?

3. He splashes on what?

4. Where does the bug jump?

Answer Key

1. in the tub

2. a bug

3. the rug

4. in the tub

Sequence Cards

I scrub myself in the tub.

A bug looks at me.

I splash on the rug.

The bug jumps in the tub.

Comprehension Card

Directions: Read the story and answer the questions.

Bedtime

At bedtime, Joe's father reads a story to him. His father tucks Joe in his covers. Then they tell each about their day. Joe always has sweet dreams!

1. Who is the story about?

2. What is the first thing father does?

3. When does the story take place?

4. Where does the story take place?

5. How does Joe sleep?

Answer Key

1. Joe and his father

2. reads Joe a story

3. at bedtime

4. Joe's bedroom

5. sleeps with sweet dreams

Sequence Cards

Joe's father reads a story to him.

His father tucks Joe in his covers.

They tell each about their day.

Joe has sweet dreams.

Directions: Read the story and answer the questions.

Lemonade for Sale!

On a hot, dry, Saturday morning in June, Amy and Melanie mixed lemonade in a plastic pitcher. They put the lemonade stand in front of their house. They sold the lemonade drinks for one quarter each. Ten children and two adults bought the cold lemonade. Amy and Melanie each needed one dollar to get into the movies. Hooray! They were on their way!

1. Who is this story about?

2. What do they sell?

3. When do they open their lemonade stand?

4. Where do they open their lemonade stand?

5. How much is a glass of lemonade?

6. Do they get to go to the movies?

Answer Key

1. The story is about Amy and Melanie.

2. They sell lemonade drinks.

3. They open on a hot, dry, Saturday morning in June.

4. They open the lemonade stand in front of their house.

5. A glass of lemonade is one quarter.

6. Yes, they get to go to the movies.

Sequence Cards

Amy and Melanie mixed lemonade
in a plastic pitcher.

They put the lemonade stand
in front of their house.

They sold the lemonade drinks
for one quarter each.

Ten children and two adults
bought the cold lemonade.

Amy and Melanie were on their
way to the movies.

Comprehension Card

Table of Contents

1. What is this page about?

2. On what page would you find the rules for football?

3. On what page would you find football equipment?

4. In what chapter would you find how to throw a football?

Answer Key

1. Table of Contents

2. Page 36

3. Page 47

4. Chapter 2

Order It!

Skill

- Students will recognize the correct order of words in sentences or paragraphs.

Student Grouping

- whole group (*Note:* Make multiple copies of sentence or paragraph strips for each student.)
- small group
- partners
- center
- independent

Materials

- Sentence Strips (page 169 or page 171) or Paragraph Strips (page 173 or page 175)
- Answer Key (Sentences) on page 167 or Answer Key (Paragraphs) on page 166
- paper and pencil

Directions

1. Choose the appropriate level of sentence or paragraph strips. If you are using the sentence strips, cut the words up and store each sentence in a small, plastic bag. Store the paragraph strips in a large, plastic bag. Or, you may copy the appropriate strips for each student.

2. Remind students what makes a sentence or a paragraph. (sentence = capital at the beginning, the sentence has to make sense, ending punctuation mark; paragraph = topic sentence, supporting details, and a concluding sentence)

3. Tell students that you are going to give them a sentence or paragraph in mixed-up order. Tell them that their job is to place them back in order.

4. Mix up the strips and allow students to place the strips in order.

5. Once the sentence or paragraph is in order, have students read the sentence or paragraph to a friend to check if it makes sense.

6. Have students check the Answer Key to make sure they have the correct order.

7. Then have students record the sentence or paragraph on a piece of paper.

Ideas

- Laminate Sentence Strips and Paragraph Strips for durability, especially when using at a center.
- Store each sentence strip or the paragraph strips in a plastic bag.
- Have students make their own sentence strips or paragraph strips. Then have them see if a friend can place the strips back in order.

Answer Key (Paragraphs)

Paragraph 1

My House

Our house has rooms I really like.

My favorite room is the family room.

My second favorite room is the kitchen.

Last, my bedroom is a great place to be.

With all these rooms, I feel really lucky.

Paragraph 2

Rainy Days

I do not like rainy days.

First of all, it makes me get wet.

Then the clouds make things dreary.

Finally, the mud gets everything dirty.

Rain can ruin an otherwise good day.

#3173 Language Arts Literacy Activities

Answer Key (Sentences)

| I | know | how | to | read | . |

| Would | you | like | some | milk | ? |

| My | friend | plays | ball | with | me | . |

| Mom | baked | a | white | cake | . |

| Who | ate | the | cookies | ? |

| There | are | many | tall | buildings | in | the | city | . |

| I | found | an | egg | in | the | bird's | nest | . |

| David | said, | "Can | I | talk | to | you?" |

| My | brother | has | a | large, | shaggy | dog | . |

| It's | John's | birthday | on | June | 12, | 2004. |

#3173 Language Arts Literacy Activities

#3173 Language Arts Literacy Activities

Sentence Strips

Strip 1: I | know | how | to | read | .

Strip 2: Would | you | like | some | milk | ?

Strip 3: My | friend | plays | ball | with | me | .

Strip 4: Mom | baked | a | white | cake | .

Strip 5: Who | ate | the | cookies | ?

Sentence Strips

There are many tall buildings in the city .

I found an egg in the bird's nest .

David said, "Can I talk to you?"

My brother has a large, shaggy dog .

It's John's birthday on June 12, 2004.

#3173 Language Arts Literacy Activities

#3173 Language Arts Literacy Activities

©*Teacher Created Resources, Inc.*

My House

Our house has rooms I really like.

My favorite room is the family room.

My second favorite room is the kitchen.

Last, my bedroom is a great place to be.

With all these rooms, I feel really lucky.

Rainy Days

I do not like rainy days.

First of all, it makes me get wet.

Then the clouds make things dreary.

Finally, the mud gets everything dirty.

Rain can ruin an otherwise good day.